I0002748

Python guide for complete beginners

by Antun Peicevic
First edition
Technical editor: Marko Maslac
Copyright© 2016 Geek University Press

Disclaimer

This book is designed to provide information about selected topics for the Python programming language. Every effort has been made to make this book as complete and as accurate as possible, but no warranty is implied. The information is provided on an as is basis. Neither the authors, Geek University Press, nor its resellers, or distributors will be held liable for any damages caused or alleged to be caused either directly or indirectly by this book. The opinions expressed in this book belong to the author and are not necessarily those of Geek University Press.

Trademarks

Geek University is a trademark of Signum Soft, LLC, and may not be used without written permission.

Feedback Information

At Geek University Press, our goal is to create in-depth technical books of the highest quality and value. Readers' feedback is a natural continuation of this process. If you have any comments about how we could improve our books and learning resources for you, you can contact us through email at books@geek-university.com. Please include the book title in your message. For more information about our books, visit our website at http://geek-university.com.

About the author

Antun Peicevic is a systems engineer with more than 10 years of experience in the internetworking field. His certifications include CCNA Routing and Switching, CompTIA Network+, CompTIA Security+, and much more. He is the founder and editor of geek-university.com, an online education portal that offers courses that cover various aspects of the IT system administration. Antun can be reached at antun@geek-university.com.

About this book

This course teaches you how to program in Python - a general-purpose, high-level programming language widely used today. This book is designed for people without much experience in the world of programming. Although the book presumes some knowledge about computer systems in general, it is customized for beginners.

What will you learn

You will learn how to download and install Python on your Windows or Linux system. You will learn what a variable is, how to perform arithmetic operations, if statement, for loops, how to capture user input, and much more.

Table of Contents

Chapter 1 - Introduction

In this chapter we will go through the basics of Python. You will learn how to download and install Python on Windows and Linux, and all the ways you can run Python code.

Python overview

Python is a general-purpose, high-level programming language that was designed emphasize code readability, developer productivity and program portability. Python can be used to write software in a wide variety of application domains, and uses natural language elements and automates certain areas of computing systems to make the process of developing a program simple and fast. It is available for Windows, Linux, Mac OS, and many other operating systems.

Python is a great programming language for beginners. Because it was designed with code readability in mind, it is an excellent choice for beginners. Here is a list of Python major advantages over other programming languages:

- **less application development time** – Python code is usually one-third to one-fifth the size of equivalent C++ or Java code.

- **code readability** – Python code is easy to read, which means you spend less time interpreting it and more time making essential changes.

- **cost** – Python is completely free to use and distribute. You can download the entire Python system's source code for free.

- **easy to learn** – because of its simplicity and frequent usage of English keywords in the code, Python has become one of the most popular languages for teaching introductory computer science courses.

- **wide user base** – Python is used in a number of successful products. For example, most of YouTube's core functionality is written in Python and Google uses Python in its search system.

- **high salary** – Python programmers have one of the highest average salaries in the US.

Python was created by a Dutch computer programmer Guido von Rossum in 1990. It has since been developed by a large team of volunteers from around the world and is available for download for free. The most recent version of Python (as of February 2015) is **3.5.1**.

Install Python on Windows

Before you start programming, you will need to download and install Python. To do this, browse to the official download site (https://www.python.org/downloads/) and download the latest version for Windows:

The file you've downloaded contains everything you will need to get started with Python: the Python interpreter, command-line tool, IDLE application, etc. Double-click the installation file to start the installation and select whether you would like to install Python for all users or just for yourself:

Select the installation directory:

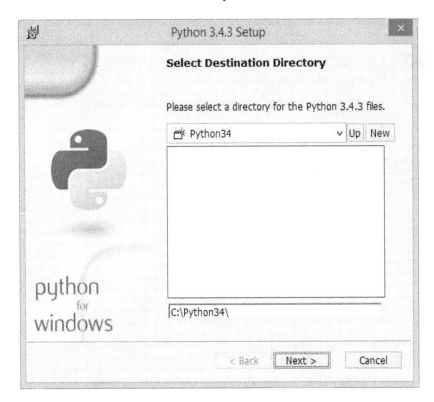

Select the Python components that will be installed. If possible, leave the defaults:

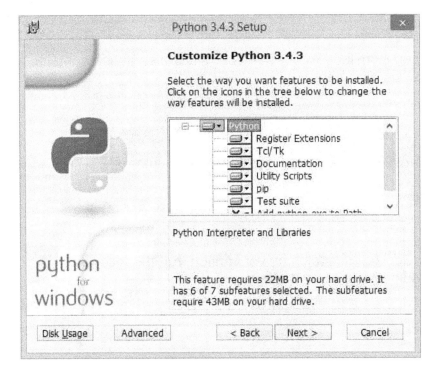

The installation should start. After it's done, click **Finish** to exit the installer:

That's it! Python is installed and ready to use.

Install Python on Linux

Most Linux distributions come with Python installed. To check if your Linux distribution contains Python, open the shell and run the following command:

```
python --version
```

You should get an output like this one, which displays the version of Python installed:

```
programmer@ubuntu:~$ python --version
Python 2.7.6
```

If you don't have Python installed or would like to install a newer version, run the following command (works in Debian-based distributions, such as **Ubuntu**):

```
sudo apt-get install python3
```

Follow the instructions to install Python.

To install Python in RPM-based distributions (e.g. SUSE) use the tools for software management included in those distributions. For example, in SUSE, you would use the **YAST** tool.

Add Python to the Windows Path

If you've installed Python in Windows using the default installation options, the path to the Python executable wasn't added to the Windows **Path variable**. The Path variable lists the directories that will be searched for executables when you type a command in the command prompt. By adding the path to the Python executable, you will be able to access **python.exe** by typing the **python** keyword (you won't need to specify the full path to the program).

Consider what happens if we enter the **python** command in the command prompt and the path to that executable is not added to the Path variable:

```
C:\>python
'python' is not recognized as an internal or external command,
operable program or batch file.
```

As you can see from the output above, the command was not found. To run **python.exe**, you need to specify the full path to the executable:

```
C:\>C:\Python34\python --version
Python 3.4.3
```

To add the path to the **python.exe** file to the Path variable, start the **Run** box and enter **sysdm.cpl**:

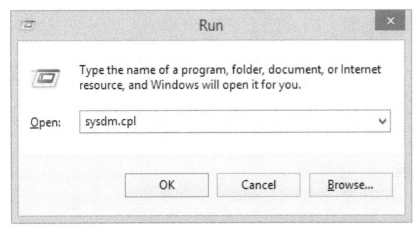

This should open up the **System Properties** window. Go to the **Advanced** tab and click the **Environment Variables** button:

In the **System variable** window, find the **Path** variable and click **Edit**:

Position your cursor at the end of the **Variable value** line and add the path to the **python.exe** file, preceded with the semicolon character (;). In our example, we have added the following value: **;C:\Python34**

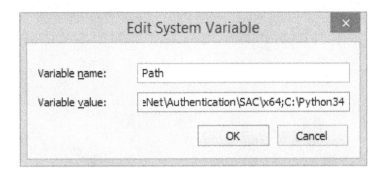

Close all windows. Now you can run **python.exe** without specifying the full path to the file:

C:>python --version

Python 3.4.3

If you get the **'python' is not recognized as an internal or external command, operable program or batch file.** error, there is something wrong with your Path variable. Note also that you will have to reopen all command prompt windows in order for changes to the Path variable take effect.

Run Python code

There are multiple ways to run the Python code. Here are the most common launching techniques:

1. the interactive prompt – this is the simplest way to run your Python programs. You simply type the code in this command-line interface. To access the interactive prompt, type **python** in the Windows command prompt or Linux shell and press **Enter**:

```
C:\>python
Python 3.4.3 (v3.4.3:9b73f1c3e601, Feb 24 2015, 22:43:06) [MSC v.1600 32 bit (In
tel)] on win32
Type "help", "copyright", "credits" or "license" for more information.
>>> print ('Hello world!')
Hello world!
>>>
```

If the **python** program is not located and you get an error message, you will need to enter the full path to the program or add its directory to the **Path** variable.

2. IDLE (Python GUI) – a graphical user interface where you can write your Python code. This **IDLE** is free and it is installed automatically during the Python installation. It enables you to edit, run, and debug Python programs in a nice GUI environment:

3. the command line – you can save your code in a file and run that file in the Windows command prompt or Linux shell. The files in which the code is saved usually have the **.py** extension. The code is run by specifying the filename after the **python** keyword:

In the picture above you can see that we've executed a file called **example.py**. If the Python directory is not listed in the PATH variable, you will need to enter the full path to the **python.exe** program.

Interactive prompt

The **interactive prompt** is the easiest way to run your Python programs – simply type the code in this command-line interface. To start the interactive prompt, type **python** from the Windows command prompt or Linux shell and press **Enter**:

If the **python** program can't be located, you need to enter the full path to the program or add its directory in the PATH variable.

After you start the interactive prompt, the information about the Python version along with some useful information about the operating system will be displayed. Below these information is the **>>>** prompt, which indicates that you're in an interactive Python interpreter session. The code you enter after the prompt will be executed once you press **Enter**. For example, to print the text **Hello world**, you can use the **print** function:

```
C:Python34>python
Python 3.4.3 (v3.4.3:9b73f1c3e601, Feb 24 2015, 22:43:06) [MSC v.1600 32 bit (In
tel)] on win32
Type "help", "copyright", "credits" or "license" for more information.
>>> print ('Hello world!')
Hello world!
```

In the example above you can see that the result of the **print** function was echoed back right away (**Hello world!**). However, the code you enter in the interactive prompt will not be saved in a file. This is why this prompt is not usually used to very often; it is usually used only for testing or experimental purposes.

You can type multiple Python commands and they will be run immediately after they are entered:

```
C:Python34>python
Python 3.4.3 (v3.4.3:9b73f1c3e601, Feb 24 2015, 22:43:06) [MSC v.1600 32 bit (Intel)] on win32
Type "help", "copyright", "credits" or "license" for more information.
>>> print ('Hello world!')
Hello world!
>>> x=5
>>> print (x)
5
>>>
```

To exit the interactive prompt, press **Ctrl+Z** on Windows or **Ctrl+D** on Linux.

IDLE editor

The **Python IDLE (Integrated DeveLopment Environment) editor** is a graphical user interface for Python development. This GUI is free and installed automatically during the Python installation. It enables you to edit, run, and debug Python programs in a simple GUI environment.

IDLE is actually a Python program that uses the standard library's **tkinter GUI toolkit** to build its windows. It is portable and can be run on all major platforms, such as Windows, Linux, Mac OS, etc. It supports the following features:

- command history and syntax colorization

- auto-indent and unindent for Python code

- word auto-completion

- support for multiple windows

- integrated debugger

The Python IDLE is usually present as an entry in the **Start button menu** in **Windows 7**. In **Windows 8**, you can run it by typing **IDLE** from the **Start menu**. Once started, it will display some useful information about the Python version and the operating system:

```
                                    Python 3.4.3 Shell                          -  □  ×

File  Edit  Shell  Debug  Options  Window  Help
Python 3.4.3 (v3.4.3:9b73f1c3e601, Feb 24 2015, 22:43:06) [MSC v.1600 32 bit (In
tel)] on win32
Type "copyright", "credits" or "license()" for more information.
>>> |
                                                                         Ln: 3 Col: 4
```

You can write your code after the **>>>** prompt and it will be executed when you press **Enter**:

```
                                    Python 3.4.3 Shell                          -  □  ×

File  Edit  Shell  Debug  Options  Window  Help
Python 3.4.3 (v3.4.3:9b73f1c3e601, Feb 24 2015, 22:43:06) [MSC v.1600 32 bit (Inte
l)] on win32
Type "copyright", "credits" or "license()" for more information.
>>> print ('Hello world!')
Hello world!
>>>
                                                                         Ln: 5 Col: 4
```

Although the shell window is useful for executing one-line commands, you will not use it to write full-fledged programs. Instead, Python IDLE comes with its own built-in text editor that you can use to write and save your code. You can start the editor by selecting **File > New File**:

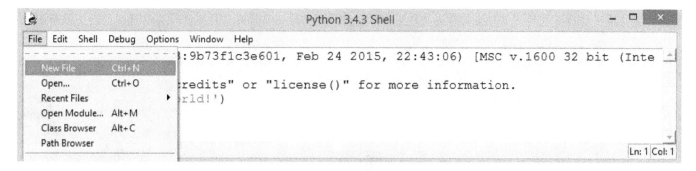

This opens up a window where you can type your code:

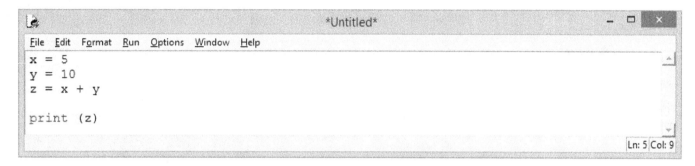

Before running your code, you will need to save it in a file (**File > Save**). Make sure that the file has the **.py** extension:

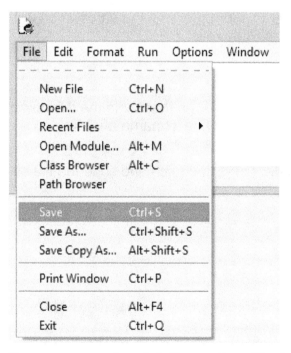

To run your code, click **Run > Run Module** (or press **F5**):

The result will be printed in the IDLE shell window:

Notice how the result of our program was displayed after the **RESTART** line.

Python IDLE is usually used by novice programmers. Later in your programming career, you will probably work with more powerful and robust tools, such as **Eclipse** or **Komodo**.

Command line

You can save your code in a file (usually with the extension **.py**) and run that file in the Windows command prompt or Linux shell. The file can be executed by specifying its name after the PYTHON keyword.

Here is an example. Type the following code in the text editor of your choice and save the file as **example.py**:

```
x = 5

y = 10

z = x + y


print (z)
```

The code above will simply add two numbers and print the result. To execute the code, open the Windows command prompt (or Linux shell) and enter PYTHON EXAMPLE.PY:

You might need to use the full path to the file **example.py** (e.g. PYTHON
C:\PYTHON34\SCRIPTS\EXAMPLE.PY). If the Python directory is not listed in the **PATH**
variable, you will also need to enter the full path to the **python.exe** program
(**C:\Python34\python.exe\example.py**).

You can provide a number of options to the **python** command. You can display them by typing
PYTHON /? in the command prompt:

For example, to display the Python version, use the python -V command:

```
C:\Python34\Scripts>python -V
Python 3.4.3
```

Help mode

Python has a feature that can provide you with information about a particular topic or command. It is called the**help mode** and can be started in the interactive mode by typing HELP ():

```
C:\Python34\Scripts>python
Python 3.4.3 (v3.4.3:9b73f1c3e601, Feb 24 2015, 22:43:06) [MSC v.1600 32 bit (In
tel)] on win32
Type "help", "copyright", "credits" or "license" for more information.
>>> help ()

Welcome to Python 3.4's help utility!

If this is your first time using Python, you should definitely check out
the tutorial on the Internet at http://docs.python.org/3.4/tutorial/.

Enter the name of any module, keyword, or topic to get help on writing
Python programs and using Python modules. To quit this help utility and
return to the interpreter, just type "quit".

To get a list of available modules, keywords, symbols, or topics, type
"modules", "keywords", "symbols", or "topics". Each module also comes
with a one-line summary of what it does; to list the modules whose name
or summary contain a given string such as "spam", type "modules spam".

help>
```

The text displayed above expains how to use the help mode. For example, to see a list of topics available, enter the TOPICS keyword:

```
help> topics


Here is a list of available topics. Enter any topic name to get more help.


ASSERTION - DELETION - LOOPING - SHIFTING

ASSIGNMENT - DICTIONARIES - MAPPINGMETHODS - SLICINGS

ATTRIBUTEMETHODS - DICTIONARYLITERALS - MAPPINGS - SPECIALATTRIBUTES

ATTRIBUTES - DYNAMICFEATURES - METHODS - SPECIALIDENTIFIERS

AUGMENTEDASSIGNMENT - ELLIPSIS - MODULES - SPECIALMETHODS

BASICMETHODS - EXCEPTIONS - NAMESPACES - STRINGMETHODS

BINARY - EXECUTION - NONE - STRINGS

BITWISE - EXPRESSIONS - NUMBERMETHODS - SUBSCRIPTS

BOOLEAN - FLOAT - NUMBERS - TRACEBACKS

CALLABLEMETHODS - FORMATTING - OBJECTS - TRUTHVALUE

CALLS - FRAMEOBJECTS - OPERATORS - TUPLELITERALS

CLASSES - FRAMES - PACKAGES - TUPLES

CODEOBJECTS - FUNCTIONS - POWER - TYPEOBJECTS

COMPARISON - IDENTIFIERS - PRECEDENCE - TYPES

COMPLEX - IMPORTING - PRIVATENAMES - UNARY

CONDITIONAL - INTEGER - RETURNING - UNICODE

CONTEXTMANAGERS - LISTLITERALS - SCOPING

CONVERSIONS - LISTS - SEQUENCEMETHODS

DEBUGGING - LITERALS - SEQUENCES


help>
```

If you want to display more information about a particular topic, simply type the name of the topic and press**Enter**. For example, to found out more about the topic **NUMBERS**, enter the NUMBERS keyword (make sure to type the word in uppercase):

```
help> NUMBERS
Numeric literals
****************
```

There are three types of numeric literals: integers, floating point numbers, and imaginary numbers. There are no complex literals (complex numbers can be formed by adding a real number and an imaginary number).

Note that numeric literals do not include a sign; a phrase like "-1" is actually an expression composed of the unary operator "'-'" and the literal "1".

Related help topics: INTEGER, FLOAT, COMPLEX, TYPES

help>

The help mode can be useful if you encounter some code you don't know the purpose of. For example, to find out what **sys.platform** means, type it inside the help mode:

```
help> sys.platform
Help on str in sys object:

sys.platform = class str(object)
| str(object='') -> str
| str(bytes_or_buffer[, encoding[, errors]]) -> str
|
| Create a new string object from the given object. If encoding or
| errors is specified, then the object must expose a data buffer
| that will be decoded using the given encoding and error handler.
| Otherwise, returns the result of object.__str__() (if defined)
| or repr(object).
| encoding defaults to sys.getdefaultencoding().
| errors defaults to 'strict'.

.

.

.

.
```

To leave the help mode, press **Enter** once.

Chapter 2 - Basic programs

In this chapter you will learn how to write your first program. We will describe variables and their data types and explain what strings are.

Write your first program

In this lesson, you will use **Python IDLE** to write your first program. Start **IDLE** and you should get a shell window, where you can write and execute commands. Traditionally, the first program you write is a program that prints the words **Hello world!**. To do that in Python, you can use the **print ()** function. This function will print text in quotes within the parentheses. So, to type **Hello world!** to the screen, you use the following command:

```
print ('Hello world!')
```

Here is the output of the command in IDLE:

```
Python 3.4.3 (v3.4.3:9b73f1c3e601, Feb 24 2015, 22:43:06) [MSC v.1600 32 bit (Intel)] on win32
Type "copyright", "credits" or "license()" for more information.
>>> print ('Hello world!')
Hello world!
>>>
```

Since the Python shell window of Python IDLE is interactive, the result of the command (**Hello world!**) was echoed back to the screen. This was nice, but what if we want to save our code? Well, Python IDLE offers another window, called the **Edit window**, where you can write the code and save it in a file, which can then be executed.

To open an Edit window, select **File > New File** from the IDLE shell window:

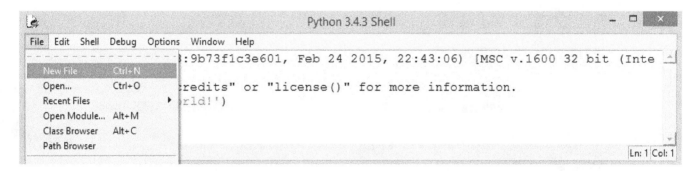

This opens up a new window where you can write code. Enter the same code as above:

```
print ('Hello world!')
```

Save the file by selecting **File > Save**. The extension of the file should be **.py**:

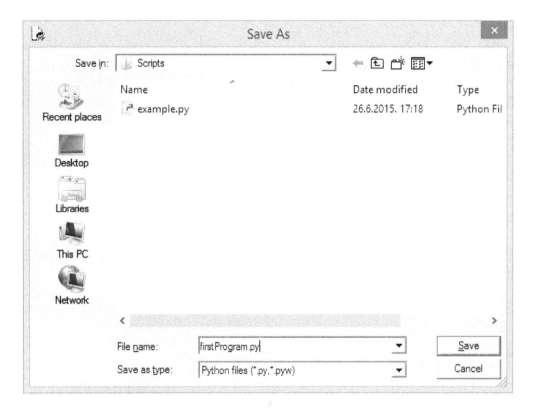

To run the program, simply click **Run > Run Module**:

The result of the program will be shown in the shell window, after the **RESTART** line:

```
Python 3.4.3 (v3.4.3:9b73f1c3e601, Feb 24 2015, 22:43:06) [MSC v.1600 32 bit (In
tel)] on win32
Type "copyright", "credits" or "license()" for more information.
>>> print ('Hello world!')
Hello world!
>>> print ("Hello world!")
Hello world!
>>> ============================== RESTART ==============================
>>>
Hello world!
>>>
```

You can use both single and double quotes for the text inside the parentheses in the **print** function.

Use comments

You can use **comments** in your Python source code in order to document it. With comments, you can remind yourself what a specific portion of the code does and make your code more accessible to other developers.

Since comments are written inside a file that is going to be executed, Python needs some way to determine that the text you write is a comment, and not a command that needs to be executed. You can mark a text as a comment in two ways:

1. using the hash-mark sign (#) – text that appears after the **#** sign will be defined as a comment and will not be executed. Consider the following code:

```
# This is a comment.

print ('Hello world!') # This is another comment.
```

When we execute the code above, we get the following output:

```
>>>

Hello world!

>>>
```

Notice how only the **print** function was executed. Python has ignored everything after the **#** sign.

2. using the three double quotes – if you need to comment out a longer multiline text, you can use three double quotes. Python will treat all text inside the three quotes as a comment. Here is an example:

```
"""

This is our first program.

It prints the text Hello world! to the screen.

It's not much, but hey, it's something.

"""

print ('Hello world!')
```

The result will be the same as above:

```
>>>

Hello world!

>>>
```

What are variables?

In programming, **variables** are storage locations that are used to store information that can later be referenced and manipulated. You can consider a variable as a sort of a container where you store an information that can later be accessed with the variable name.

In Python, variables are created when they are first assigned values. Values are assigned using the assignment operator (**=**). For example, to create a variable named **x** and store the numeric value of **3** in it, you can use the following command:

```
x = 3
```

The command above does three things:

1. Creates an object that will represent the value **3**.
2. Creates the variable **x**.
3. Links the variable **x** to the new object **3**.

You can now use the variable **x** in your code. For example, to print the content of the variable, you can use the following command:

```
>>> print (x)

3
```

Notice how you didn't need to write quotes around the variable name. When you want to print the content of a variable, quotes are not used. Consider what would happen if you use quotes:

```
>>> print ('x')

x
```

Python considers the text inside the quotes to be a string and not a variable name. That is why the letter **x** was printed, and not the content of the variable **x**.

Once declared, the value of a variable can be changed:

```
>>> x = 3

>>> print (x)

3

>>>

>>> x = 5

>>> print (x)

5

>>>
```

Notice how the first print function printed the value of **3**. We have then changed the value of the variable **x** to **5**. The second print function printed the value of **5**.

Variable data types

Variables in Python can be of a different **data type**. The data type of a variable is important because it specifies the kind of information that can be stored inside a variable. For example, to store numeric information, you need a variable of the numeric type. You can't store a string in a variable designed to store numeric information. You will need to create a variable of the string type to store a string.

There are five standard data types in Python:

- **numbers** – used to store numeric values. Numbers can be stored as integers, long integers, floating-point values, and complex numbers. For example, the statement **x = 5** will store the integer number **5** in the variable **x**.

- **strings** – used to store a contiguous set of characters. To define a string, you type the characters within single or double quotes. For example, **newString = 'This is a text'** will store that string of characters (**This is a text**) in the variable **newString**.

- **lists** – similar to **arrays** in some other programming languages, lists in Python are used to store a set of elements under a single variable name. Each element can be accesses by using its index, which is simply an address that identifies the item's place in the list. Elements of a list are defined inside the square brackets (**[]**) and are separated by commas. For example. the **myNumbers = [5,3,2,1]** statement will define the list**myNumbers** with four elements. To access the first element of the list (the number **5**), we can specify its index in the square brackets. Since indexes start from **0**, to access the first element of the list, we would use the following statement: **myNumbers[0]**.

- **tuples** – similar to lists, tuples in Python are used to store a set of elements under a single variable name. However, unlike lists, they cannot be changed once created. You can thought of tuples as read-only lists. They are used to represent fixed collections of elements, like days in the week. Elements of a tuple are defined inside the parentheses and separated by commas. For example, the **myNumbers = (2,4,2,5)** will create a tuple with four elements. To access the first element, we use the **myNumbers[0]** statement.

- **dictionaries** – also known as **mappings**, dictionaries are used to store a set of objects, but they store objects by key instead by relative position. The elements are defined within the curly braces. For example, the statement **myDict = {'color' : 'blue', 'size' : 'small'}** will create a two word dictionary. We can access the elements of this dictionary by specifying a key. To access the value associated with the key **color**, we would use the following statement: **myDict['color']**.

Numeric variables

Numeric variables in Python are used to store numbers. Numbers are usually stored as integers, floating-point values, or complex numbers, depending on the requirements of the program. For a start, we will describe the most common types – integer and floating-point values.

Integers

Integers are whole numbers, such as 1, 20, 3000, 10200305, etc. They are declared simply by writing a whole number. For example, the statement **x = 5** will store the integer number **5** in the variable **x**. For **64-bit** platforms, you can store any whole numbers between –**9223372036854775808** and **9223372036854775807** in an integer variable in Python.

In Python 3.x, **integer** and **long** were merged into a single **integer** type. In Python 2.x, they were two different data types.

Floating-point values

Numbers with a decimal portion are **floating-point values**. They are declared by writing a number with a decimal part. For example, the statement **x=5.3** will store the floating-point value **5.3** in the variable **x**. You can store incredibly large numbers, ranging from **2.2250738585072014 x 10308** to **1.7976931348623157 x 10308**.

You can convert an integer number to a floating-point value using the FLOAT (NUMBER) function, like in this example:

```
x = 5
print (x)


print (float (x))
```

When executed, the code above produces the following output:

```
>>>
5
5.0
>>>
```

To convert a floating-point value to an integer number, use the INT(NUMBER) function.

Now, consider what happens if we divide two integer numbers:

```
>>> x = 5
>>> y = 2
>>> z = x / y
>>> print (z)
2.5
```

```
>>>
```

Notice how, although numbers are defined as **integers** (whole numbers), the result of the division operation was a **floating-point** number. This is a **Python 3.x** feature – **Python 2.x** would perform integer division and return the result of **2**.

Strings

Strings in Python can be used to store a contiguous set of characters. To define a string, you simple type the characters within single or double quotes. For example, **newString = 'Hello world!'** will store that string of characters (**Hello world!**) in the variable called **newString**:

```
>>> newString = 'Hello world!'
>>> print (newString)
Hello world!
```

You will get the same result if you use the double quotes to define a string:

```
>>> newString = "Hello world!"
>>> print (newString)
Hello world!
```

The reason why both forms are used is so you can embed a quote character of the other type inside a string. For example, you may embed a single-quote character in a string enclosed in double-quote characters:

```
>>> newString = "Mark's car"
>>> print (newString)
Mark's car
```

Note that you can not perform numeric operations with string variables, even if the string stored in the variable consists only of numbers. Consider the following example:

```
>>> x = '5'
>>> y = '3'
>>> print (x + y)
53
```

The **+** operator concatenates two strings. To perform an arithmetic operation, we need to conver the string variables to integer or floating-point variables:

```
>>> x = int ('5')
>>> y = int ('3')
```

```
>>> print (x + y)
8
```

Get the current date and time

You can get the current date and time using Python. However, you will need to import a module called **datetime**. To do this, we need to use a single statement – IMPORT DATETIME. Here's the code to get the current date and time in Python:

```
import datetime
currentDate = datetime.datetime.now()
print (currentDate)
```

The code above produces the following output when executed:

```
>>>
1997-06-29 14:56:08.800197
>>>
```

To get only the current date, you can use the following code:

```
import datetime
currentDate = datetime.datetime.now().date()
print (currentDate)
```

Here is the output:

```
>>>
1997-06-29
>>>
```

To obtain the current time, you can use the TIME() command:

```
import datetime
currentDate = datetime.datetime.now().time()
print (currentDate)
```

The output:

```
>>>
14:57:47.801347
```

Chapter 3 - Operators overview

In this chapter we will describe different types of operators found in Python: arithmetic, comparison, logical, assignment, membership, and identity operators.

Arithmetic operators

The arithmetic operators in Python are used to perform math operations, such as addition, subtraction, multiplication, and division. Python also offers a number of libraries that enable you to perform more complex math tasks.

Here is a list of the arithmetic operators in Python:

- **Addition (+)** – adds two values together. Example: 3 + 2 = 5.

- **Subtraction (-)** – subtracts right hand operand from the left hand operand. 3 – 2 = 1.

- **Multiplication (*)** – multiplies the right operand by the left operand. Example: 3 * 4 = 12.

- **Division (/)** – divides the left operand by the right operand. Example: 9 / 3 = 3.

- **Modulus (%)** – divides the left operand by the right operand and returns the remainder. Example: 9 % 5 = 4.

- **Exponent (**)** – calculates the exponential value. Example: 3 ** 4 = 81.

- **Floor Division (//)** – performs integer division. Example: 9//2 = 4.

You are probably familiar with all operators mentioned above, except the **modulus operator** (%). The concept is actually simple – the modulus operator returns the remainder after integer division. Consider the following example:

20 % 3

The integer division of the numbers above will give the result of **6**.
6 * 3 = 18.
This gives a reminder of **2** (**18 + 2 = 20**).

Another example:

5 % 2

Integer division = **2**.
2*2 = 4.
The remider is **1**. So **5 % 2 = 1**.

One more example:

13 % 5

Integer division = **2**
2 * 5 = 10
The reminder is **3**.

Comparison operators

As their name suggests, the **comparison operators** in Python are used to compare one value to another. The result of a comparison is a **Boolean** value, which can be either **True** or **False**. The following comparison operators exist in Python:

- **==** – determines whether two values are equal. Examples: 1 == 1 is True, 1 == 2 is False.

- **!=** – determines whether two values are not equal. Examples: 1 != 2 returns True, 1 != 1 returns False.

- **>** – determines if the value of the left operand is greater than the value of the right operand. Examples: 3 > 1 is True, 1 > 2 is False.

- **<** – determines if the value of the left operand is less than the value of the right operand. Examples: 1 < 2 is True, 3 < 2 is False.

- **>=** – determines if the value of the left operand is greater than or equal to the value of the right operand. Examples: 3 >= 1 is True, 1 >= 2 is False.

- **<=** – determines if the value of the left operand is less than or equal to the value of the right operand. Examples: 1 <= 3 is True, 3 <= 2 is False.

Here are a couple of examples:

```
>>> x = 5
>>> y = 7
>>> x == y
False
>>> x != y
True
>>> x > y
False
>>> x < y
True
>>> x >= y
False
>>> x <= y
True
>>> x + y == 12
True
```

```
>>> x + y < 15
True
>>> x + y > 20
False
>>> x + y <= 12
True
```

Logical operators

The **logical operators** in Python are used to combine the **true** or **false** values of variables (or expressions) so you can figure out their resultant truth value. Three logical operators are available in Python:

1. and – returns **True** only if both operands are true. In any other case, **False** will be returned. For example, the following expression will evaluate to True: **5 < 7 and 5 > 3**, because 5 is indeed less than 7 and greater than 3. Here is the **and operator's truth table** (a table that lists all the possible inputs and the results for the logical operators):

and operator's truth table

First operand	Second operand	Result
True	True	True
True	False	False
False	True	False
False	False	False

Here are a couple of examples:

```
>>> 5 < 7 and 5 > 3
True
>>>
>>> 3 > 3 and 55 > 30
False
>>> 15 / 3 >= 200 and 3 == 3
False
>>> 55 == 55 and 3 <= 3
True
```

2. or – returns **True** when one or both of the operands are true. For example, the expression **5 < 3 or 3 == 3** will return **True** because the second operand (**3 == 3**) evaluates to **True**. Only if both operands are false will **False** be returned. The truth table for this operator looks like this:

or operator's truth table

First operand	Second operand	Result
True	True	True
True	False	True
False	True	True
False	False	False

Examples:

```
>>> 3 == 3 or 5 < 3
True
>>> 15 < 3 or 5 > 3
True
>>> 12 <= 1 or 5 < 1
False
>>> 20 + 3 >= 23 or 5 != 5
True
```

3. not – negates the truth value of a single operand. In other words, **True** becomes **False** and vice versa. The truth table here is smaller because only a single operand is used:

not operator's truth table

Operand	Result
True	False
False	True

Examples:

```
>>> not True
False
>>> not False
True
>>> not 5 > 3
```

False

>>> not (5 > 3 and 5 > 2)

False

>>> not (5 > 3 and 5 < 33)

False

>>> not (5 < 3 and 5 < 33)

True

Let's expain the last example – **not (5 < 3 and 5 < 33)** – and why it returns **True**. Simply evaluate the expression in the parentheses first:

5 < 3 – 5 isn't smaller than 3, so this expression is **false**.
5 < 33 – 5 is smaller than 33, so this expression is **true**.

From the truth table for the **and** operator above, we know that **False** and **True** return **False**. So the expression **5 < 3 and 5 < 33** will return **False**. Now, we just need to apply the **not** operator, so **False** becomes **True**.

Assignment operators

The **assignment operators** in Python are used to store data into a variable. We've already used the most common assingment operator (**=**), but there are many more of them:

- **=** – assigns the value found in the right operands to the left operand. Example: x = 5.

- **+=** – adds the value found in the right operand to the value found in the left operand. Example: x = 5, x += 3 results in x = 8.

- **-=** – substracts the value of the right operand from the value found in the left operand. Example: x = 5, x -= 3 results in x = 2.

- ***=** – multiplies the value of the right operand by the value of the left operand. Example: x = 5, x *= 3 results in x = 15.

- **/=** – divides the value of the left operand by the value of the right operand. Example: x = 5, x /=3 results in x = 1.667.

- **%=** – divides the value found in the left operand by the value found in the right operand. The reminder will be placed in the left operand. Example: x = 5, x %=3 results in x = 2.

- ****=** – determines the exponential value found in the left operand when raised to the power of the value in the right operand. Example: x = 5, x **=3 results in x = 125.

- **//=** – divides the value found in the left operand by the value of the right operand. The integer result will be placed in the left operand. Example: x = 5, x //= 3 results in x = 1.

Membership operators

The **membership operators** in Python are used to test whether a value is found within a sequence. For example, you can use the membership operators to test for the presence of a substring in a string. Two membership operators exist in Python:

- **in** – evaluates to **True** if the value in the left operand appears in the sequence found in the right operand. For example, **'Hello' in 'Hello world'** returns **True** because the substring **Hello** is present in the string **Hello world!**.

- **not in** – evaluates to **True** if the value in the left operand doesn't appear in the sequence found in the right operand. For example, **'house' in 'Hello world'** returns **True** because the substring **house** is not present in the string **Hello world!**.

Here are a couple of examples:

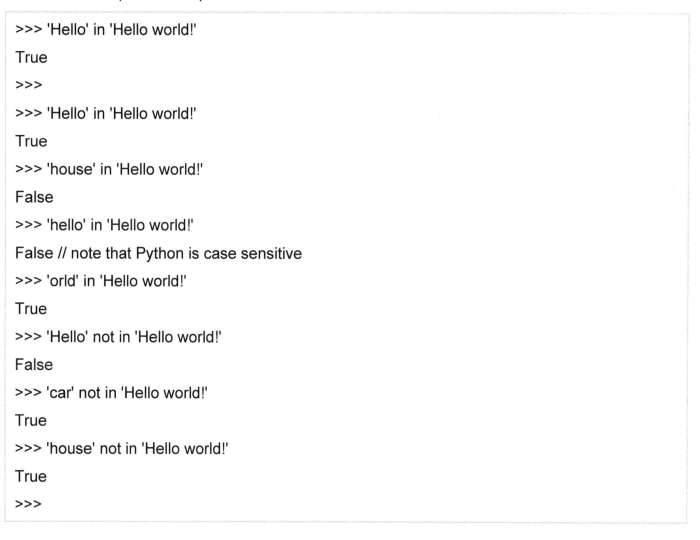

```
>>> 'Hello' in 'Hello world!'
True
>>>
>>> 'Hello' in 'Hello world!'
True
>>> 'house' in 'Hello world!'
False
>>> 'hello' in 'Hello world!'
False // note that Python is case sensitive
>>> 'orld' in 'Hello world!'
True
>>> 'Hello' not in 'Hello world!'
False
>>> 'car' not in 'Hello world!'
True
>>> 'house' not in 'Hello world!'
True
>>>
```

Identity operators

The **identity operators** in Python are used to determine whether a value is of a certain class or type. They are usually used to determine the type of data a certain variable contains. For example, you can combine the identity operators with the built-in TYPE() function to ensure that you are working with the specific variable type.

Two identity operators are available in Python:

- **is** – returns **True** if the type of the value in the right operand points to the same type in the left operand. For example, TYPE(3) IS INT evaluates to **True** because **3** is indeed an integer number.

- **is not** – returns **True** if the type of the value in the right operand points to a different type than the value in the left operand. For example, TYPE(3) IS NOT FLOAT evaluates to **True** because **3** is not a floating-point value.

Here are a couple of examples:

```
>>> x = 5
>>> type(x) is int
True
>>> type(x) is not float
True
>>> y = 3.23
>>> type(y) is not float
False
>>> type(y) is int
False
```

Chapter 4 - Conditional statements

In this chapter we will describe conditional statements. You will learn how to get user input and use logical operators in your programs.

The if statement

The easiest method for making a decision in Python is by using the **if statement**. The if statement enables you to select the actions to perform if the evaluated condition is true. The syntax of the if statement is:

```
if condition:
    statements
```

As you can see, the **if statement** begins with the word **if**. After the **if** keyword comes a **condition** that will be evaluated. The condition must end with a **colon** (**:**). After the condition come the **statements** that will be perfomed if the **condition** evaluates to **true**. Note that the text indentation is important in **if statements** and affects the meaning of code, so make sure to indent the statements.

Consider the following example:

```
x = 5


if x == 5:
    print ('Hello world!')
```

In the example above the value of **x** is set to **5**. The **if** statement will evaluate whether the **x = 5** and print **Hello world!** if the condition is evaluated to true. Because **x** indeed is **5**, the text **Hello world!** will be printed.

Note that we've used the **equality operator** (**==**), and not the assignment operator (**=**) to evaluate the condition. The equality operator checks whether the two values are equal.

Here is another example:

```
x = 5


if x == 6:
    print ('Hello world!')
```

In the example above the text will not be printed because **x** is not equal to **6**.

One more example:

```
myName = 'Mark'


if myName == 'Mark':
    print ('Hi Mark!')
```

In this case, the text **Hi Mark!** will be printed because the variable **myName** indeed holds the string **Mark**:

```
>>>
Hi Mark!
>>>
```

Get user input

Most of the applications you write will need some way to interact with a user. The simplest way to obtain user input is by using the INPUT() function. This function prompts the user for an input from the keyboard. Once the user has give the input and pressed **Enter**, the program flow continues.

Here is an example:

```
myName = input('What is your name? ')


print ('Hello', myName)
```

The code above will produce the following output:

```
>>>
What is your name? Mark
Hello Mark
>>>
```

The INPUT() function will always output a string. If you want a number, you will need to convert the user input to a number using functions such as INT(VARIABLE) or FLOAT(VARIABLE).

Another example of the INPUT() function:

```
x = 5
y = int(input('Type a number: '))


z = x + y


print (y, 'plus 5 equals', z)
```

The output of the code above:

```
>>>
Type a number: 3
3 plus 5 equals 8
>>>
```

One more example:

```
name = input('What is your name? ')
x = int(input('How old are you? '))


if x >= 21:
    print (name,'you are old enough.')
```

The output, if we enter the name **Mark** and the number **22**:

```
What is your name? Mark
How old are you? 22
Mark you are old enough.
```

The if...else statement

The **if...else statement** in Python is used when you need to choose between one of two alternatives. The **else**clause in the code will be executed if the condition for the **if** statement isn't met, which allows you to perform an alternative task. The syntax of the **if...else** statement is:

```
if condition:
     statements
else:
     statements
```

Consider the following example:

```
name = input('What is your name? ')
x = int(input('How old are you? '))


if x >= 21:
    print(name,'you are old enough.')
```

```
else:
    print(name,'you are not old enough.')
```

Here is what happens if we enter the values **Mark** and **19**:

```
What is your name? Mark

How old are you? 19

Mark you are not old enough.
```

In the example above the user is prompted to enter the name and age. The **if** statement will than evaluate whether the user if **21** or older and print the corresponding message. If the user enter a number less than **21**, the**else** statement will be executed and the corresponding message will be printed. Note that the **else** statement will be executed only if the **if** statement evaluates to **false.** If the user enters a number greater or equal to **21**, the code under the **else** statement will not be executed.

Here is another example:

```
x = int(input('Enter a number: '))


if x % 2 == 0: # checks whether the number is divisible by 2.
    print('The number you have entered is an even number.')
else:
    print('The number you have entered is an odd number.')
```

The output:

```
Enter a number: 5

The number you have entered is an odd number.

>>>

Enter a number: 67

The number you have entered is an odd number.

>>>

Enter a number: 100

The number you have entered is an even number.
```

The if…elif statement

The **if…elif** statement in Python is used when you need to choose between more than two alternatives. The **elifclause** can be used to create a number of conditions that can be evaluated. The syntax of the statement is:

```
if condition:

      statements

elif condition:

      statements

elif condition:

      statements

      .

      .

      .

else:

      statements
```

Consider the following example:

```
print('Available cars: ')

print('1.BMW')

print('2.Ford')

print('3.Tesla')

print('4.Chrysler')

print('5.Toyota')


x = int(input('Select your car: '))


if x == 1:

    print('You have selected BMW.')

elif x == 2:

    print('You have selected Ford.')

elif x == 3:

    print('You have selected Tesla.')
```

```
elif x == 4:
    print('You have selected Chrysler.')
elif x == 5:
    print('You have selected Toyota.')
else:
    print ('Invalid selection.')
```

Here is the output:

```
Available cars:
1.BMW
2.Ford
3.Tesla
4.Chrysler
5.Toyota
Select your car: 2
You have selected Ford.
```

The example above begins by displaying a menu. A user is prompted to make a selection by entering a number between **1** and **5**. The user's selection is then evaluated. If the user enters anything other then these numbers, the**Invalid selection** message will be displayed.

Nested if statements

You can place an **if** (or **if…else**, **if…elif**) statement inside another statement. This process is called **nesting** and enables you to make complex decisions based on different inputs. Here is a sample syntax:

```
if condition:
    if condition:
        statements
    else:
        statements
else:
    statements
```

Note how the lines above are indented. The indentation is important because it informs Python that the indentent statement is the second-level statement.

Consider the following example:

```
x = int(input('Enter your age: '))


if x > 21:
    if x > 100:
        print('You are too old, go away!')
    else:
        print('Welcome, you are of the right age!')
else:
    print('You are too young, go away!')
```

The program above prompts the user to enter his age. The program will first determine if the user is older than **21**. If that is the case, the program will additionally check if the user is older than **100**. If that is the case, it will print the corresponding message, indicating that the user is too old. If the user entered a number between **21** and **100**, the **Welcome, you are of the right age!** message will be printed. If the user has entered a number less than **21**, he will be informed that he is too young. Note that the nested **if...else** statement will not be executed at all if the user has entered a value less than **21**.

The output of the example above:

```
Enter your age: 55

Welcome, you are of the right age!

>>>

Enter your age: 13

You are too young, go away!

>>>

Enter your age: 101

You are too old, go away!

>>>
```

You can also nest a statement inside a nested statement. Just make sure to indent your code properly.

Use logical operators

The **logical operators** in Python (**and**, **or**, **not**) are often used in the **if**, **if...else**, and **if...elif** statements. They enable you to make multiple comparisons inside a single statement, such as to determine whether a value is within a certain range. Consider the following example:

```
x = int(input('Enter your age: '))


if x < 21 or x > 100:
    print('You are too young or too old, go away!')
else:
    print('Welcome, you are of the right age!')
```

Here is the output of the various inputs:

```
Enter your age: 14
You are too young or too old, go away!
>>>
Enter your age: 101
You are too young or too old, go away!
>>>
Enter your age: 25
Welcome, you are of the right age!
>>>
```

The code above checks to see if the user has entered a value less than **21** or greated than **101** (**if x < 21 or x > 100**) and if that is the case, informs the user that she is too young or too old. If the user enters any other number between **21** and **100**, the **Welcome, you are of the right age!** message will be displayed.

Here is another example:

```
x = int(input('Enter your age: '))


if x > 0 and x < 21:
    print('Oww, you are still a child!')
elif x > 21 and x < 40:
    print('You are so young!')
elif x > 40 and x < 60:
    print('You are not that young, but not that old also!')
elif x > 60 and x < 100:
    print ('Golden ages!')
```

```
elif x < 0 or x > 100:
    print ('I do not really belive you that you are younger than 0 or older than 100!')
else:
    print ('Invalid selection.')
```

The code above will check the user input and print the corresponding message. For example, if the user enters the value of **45**, the **elif x > 40 and x < 60** statement will evalute to **True** and the **You are not that young, but not that old also!** message will be printed.

Here is the output:

```
Enter your age: 58
You are not that young, but not that old also!
>>>
Enter your age: 12
Oww, you are still a child!
>>>
Enter your age: 105
I do not really belive you that you are younger than 0 or older than 100!
>>>
Enter your age: -6
I do not really belive you that you are younger than 0 or older than 100!
>>>
Enter your age: 25
You are so young!
>>>
Enter your age: 68
Golden ages!
```

Chapter 5 - Loops

In this chapter we will show you what loops are. You will also learn how to use break, continue, and pass statements.

The for loop

Looping statements are used to repeat an action over and over again. One of the most common looping statements is the **for loop**. The syntax of this loop is:

```
for variable in object:
    statements
```

Here is a breakdown of the syntax:

- **for** – the keyword that indicates that the **for** statement begins.
- **variable** – specifies the name of the variable that will hold a single element of a sequence.
- **in** – indicates that the sequence comes next.
- **object** – the sequence that will be stepped through.
- **statements** – the statements that will be executed in each iteration.

Take a look at the following example:

```
for letter in 'Hello World!':
    print (letter)
```

The code above will produce the following output:

```
>>>
H
e
l
l
o

W
o
r
l
d
!
```

Let's break down the code:

- **for** – starts the **for** statement.

- **letter** – the name of the variable that will hold the current value. During the first iteration, the first item in the sequence will be assigned to the variable. During the second iteration, the second item in the sequence will be assigned to the variable, etc. In our case, the string value **H** will be assigned to the variable **letter** during the first iteration, the value **e** during the second iteration, etc.

- **sequence** – in our case, the sequence is a string of characters (**Hello world**).

- **print (letter)** – the statement that will be executed in each iteration. In our case, the letter currently stored in the variable **letter** will be printed.

for loops are usually used with the RANGE() function, explained in the next lesson.

Use for loop with the range() function

The RANGE() function in Python is often used in **for statements** to define the number of loop iterations. This built-in function creates lists containing arithmetic progressions. The syntax of the RANGE() function is:

```
range(start, stop [, step])
```

The **start** argument is the starting number. The **stop** argument is the last number (which is not included). The**step** argument is optional and defines the difference between each number in the sequence.

If the **step** argument is omitted, it defaults to **1**. If the **start** argument is omitted, it defaults to **0**. Note that all arguments have to be **integers**.

Here is an example. Let's say that we want to loop through a for loop 10 times. We can use the **range(1, 11)**function inside a for statement to do that:

```
for i in range(1, 11):
    print ('This is the', i, 'iteration.')
```

When run, the code above gives the following output:

```
>>>
This is the 1 iteration.
This is the 2 iteration.
This is the 3 iteration.
This is the 4 iteration.
```

This is the 5 iteration.

This is the 6 iteration.

This is the 7 iteration.

This is the 8 iteration.

This is the 9 iteration.

This is the 10 iteration.

\>\>\>

Notice that we didn't specify the **step** argument in the example above, so it defaulted to **1**. Also, notice that the last number is **10**, and not **11**. This is because the number defined as the **stop** argument isn't included in the range.

Here is another example, this time with the **step** argument defined:

```
for i in range(1, 11, 2):
    print ('This will print only odd numbers:', i)
```

The output:

```
>>>
This will print only odd numbers: 1
This will print only odd numbers: 3
This will print only odd numbers: 5
This will print only odd numbers: 7
This will print only odd numbers: 9
>>>
```

The break statement

The **break** statement is used to terminate a loop in Python. It is usually used inside an **if** statement that defines the condition for breaking out of the loop. The program execution is resumed at the next statement after the body of the loop.

Here is an example:

```
word = input('Type a word that is less than 5 characters long: ')
letterNumber = 1


for i in word:
    print ('Letter', letterNumber, 'is', i)
    letterNumber+=1
    if letterNumber > 5:
        print('The word you have entered is more than 5 characters long.')
        break
```

The code above will print each letter of the word you enter. If you enter a word that is more than **5** characters long, the **break** statement inside the **if** statement will end the loop after the fifth letter:

```
Type a word that is less than 5 characters long: Hello World!
Letter 1 is H
Letter 2 is e
Letter 3 is l
Letter 4 is l
Letter 5 is o
The word you have entered is more than 5 characters long.
```

Notice how only the first five letters were printed. The **break** statement ended the loop because the string was too long.

If you place a **break** statement inside a nested loop (a loop inside another loop), it will terminate the innermost loop.

The continue statement

The **continue** statement in Python is used to skip the rest of the code inside a loop for the current iteration only. What this means is that, unlike with the **break** statement, the loop does not terminate but continues on with the next iteration. The **continue** statement is usually used inside an **if** statement that defines the condition for not executing the statements inside the loop.

Here is an example:

```python
for i in range(1,11):
    if i==5:
        continue
    print (i)
```

The output:

```
>>>
1
2
3
4
6
7
8
9
10
>>>
```

The example above prints all numbers from **1** to **10** except the number **5**. This is so because when the variable i becomes equal to **5**, the **if** statement will be executed and the **continue** statement inside of it will force the program to skip the **print** statement.

Here's another example:

```python
word = input('Type a word: ')


for i in word:
    if (i == 'a' or i=='e' or i=='o' or i=='u' or i=='i'):
        continue
    print (i)
```

The program above will print the word you enter without the vowels:

```
>>>
Type a word: Hello world!
H
l
l

w
r
l
d
!
>>>
```

The pass statement

The **pass** statement in Python usually serves as a placeholder to ensure that the block has at least one statement. It is a **null operation**, which means nothing happens when it executes. In some cases, however, it can be used instead of the **continue** statement, since it allows the completition of the code inside the **if** statement in which it appears. Consider the following example:

```
for i in range(1,11):
    if i==5:
        pass
        print ('Number 5 encountered.')
    print (i)
```

The output:

```
>>>
1
2
3
4
Number 5 encountered.
5
```

```
6
7
8
9
10
>>>
```

Notice how the **Number 5 encountered** message was printed. If **continue** was used instead of the **pass**statement, the **print** statement inside the **if** statement would not execute.

Another example:

```
x = 0

for currentLetter in 'Hello world!':
    if currentLetter == 'l':
        pass
        x+=1
        print('This is the',x,'instance of the letter l.')
    print ('The current letter is', currentLetter)


print ('There have been',x,'instances of letter l.')
```

The code above calculates how many times the letter **l** appears in the **Hello world!** string and produces the following output:

```
>>>
The current letter is H
The current letter is e
This is the 1 instance of the letter l.
The current letter is l
This is the 2 instance of the letter l.
The current letter is l
The current letter is o
The current letter is
The current letter is w
```

The current letter is o

The current letter is r

This is the 3 instance of the letter l.

The current letter is l

The current letter is d

The current letter is !

There have been 3 instances of letter l.

>>>

Use else statement in loops

You can use the **else** statement in the **for** and **while** loops in Python. The **else** statement is optional and executes if the loop iteration completes normally. If the loop is terminated with a **break** statement, the **else** statement will not be executed.

Consider the following example:

```
for currentLetter in 'Hello world!':
   print ('The current letter is', currentLetter)
else:
   print ('All letters were printed.')
```

Here is the output:

```
>>>
The current letter is H
The current letter is e
The current letter is l
The current letter is l
The current letter is o
The current letter is
The current letter is w
The current letter is o
The current letter is r
The current letter is l
The current letter is d
```

The current letter is !

All letters were printed.

>>>

The simple example above printed all the letters in the **Hello world!** string. Because the loop iteration completed normally, the **else** statement was also executed and the text **All letters were printed.** was printed to the screen.

Now consider the example in which the code inside the **else** statement will not be executed:

```
for currentLetter in 'Hello world!':
    print ('The current letter is', currentLetter)
    if currentLetter == 'w':
        break
else:
    print ('All letters were printed.')
```

The output:

```
>>>
The current letter is H
The current letter is e
The current letter is l
The current letter is l
The current letter is o
The current letter is
The current letter is w
>>>
```

Notice how the **for** loop was terminated when the letter **w** was encountered. Because the loop iteration wasn't completed normally, the **else** statement wasn't executed.

The while loop

The **while loop** in Python is used to repeatedly execute statements as long as the given condition is true. When the condition becomes false, the program execution is resumed at the next statement after the body of the while loop. The syntax of the while loop is:

```
while condition:
    statements
```

Here is a simple example of the while loop in action:

```
x = 0

while x < 10:
    print (x)
    x+=1
```

The code above will print the value of the variable **x** as long as **x** is less than **10**. The output:

```
>>>
0
1
2
3
4
5
6
7
8
9
>>>
```

Notice how we have added **1** to **x** in each loop iteration (the **x+=1** statement). This is important because without it, the loop would be an endless loop, meaning that it would never end – the value of **x** would never increase and the loop would execute forever. Try removing the **x+=1** line and see what happens.

Here is another example:

```
x = int(input('Enter a number: '))

while x != 0:
    y = x*10
    print (x, 'times 10 equals', y)
```

```
x = int(input('Enter a number. Press 0 to quit: '))
```

The code above asks the user to enter a number and it multiply it by **10**. If the user enters **0**, the program quits:

```
Enter a number: 14

14 times 10 equals 140

Enter a number. Press 0 to quit: 54

54 times 10 equals 540

Enter a number. Press 0 to quit: 47

47 times 10 equals 470

Enter a number. Press 0 to quit: 11

11 times 10 equals 110

Enter a number. Press 0 to quit: 2

2 times 10 equals 20

Enter a number. Press 0 to quit: 14

14 times 10 equals 140

Enter a number. Press 0 to quit: 0

>>>
```

Nested loop statements

You can place a loop statement inside another loop statement. This process is called **nesting**. Consider the following example:

```
x = int(input('Enter a number: '))


while x != 0:
    for y in range (1, x):
        print (y)
        y+=1
    x = int(input('Enter a number: '))
```

The simple example above asks the user to enter a number and then prints all numbers less than that number. The process will continue until the user enters **0**:

```
>>>
```

```
Enter a number: 5
1
2
3
4
Enter a number: 12
1
2
3
4
5
6
7
8
9
10
11
Enter a number: 0
>>>
```

Chapter 6 - Errors

In this chapter you will learn how to deal with errors in your code. You will learn different types of errors, and how you can catch specific exceptions.

Types of errors

Errors in Python can be categorized into two types:

1. Compile time errors – errors that occur when you ask Python to run the application. Before the program can be run, the source code must be compiled into the machine code. If the conversion can not perfomed, Python will inform you that your application can not be run before the error is fixed. The most common errors of this type are syntax errors – for example, if you don't end an **if statement** with the **colon**. Here is an example:

```
x = int(input('Enter a number: '))


if x%2 == 0

    print('You have entered an even number.')
else:

    print ('You have entered an odd number.')
```

The code above checks if the number the user enters is an odd or an even number. However, notice how the **if statement** is missing the **colon** (:) at the end of the line. Because of it, the program won't run and the interpreter will even inform use what the problem is:

```
C:Python34Scripts>python error.py
File "error.py", line 3
if x%2 == 0
         ^
SyntaxError: invalid syntax
```

2. Runtime errors – errors that occur after the code has been compiled and the program is running. The error of this type will cause your program to behave unexpectedly or even crash. An example of an runtime error is the division by zero. Consider the following example:

```
x = float(input('Enter a number: '))
y = float(input('Enter a number: '))
z = x/y


print (x,'divided by',y,'equals: ',z)
```

The program above runs fine until the user enters **0** as the second number:

```
>>>
Enter a number: 9
Enter a number: 2
```

9.0 divided by 2.0 equals: 4.5

>>>

Enter a number: 11

Enter a number: 3

11.0 divided by 3.0 equals: 3.6666666666666665

>>>

Enter a number: 5

Enter a number: 0

Traceback (most recent call last):

File "C:/Python34/Scripts/error1.py", line 3, in <module>

z = x/y

ZeroDivisionError: float division by zero

>>>

Syntax and logical errors

Two types of errors can occur in Python:

1. Syntax errors – usually the easiest to spot, syntax errors occur when you make a typo. Not ending an **if**statement with the colon is an example of an syntax error, as is misspelling a Python keyword (e.g. using **whille**instead of **while**). Syntax error usually appear at compile time and are reported by the interpreter. Here is an example of a syntax error:

```
x = int(input('Enter a number: '))


whille x%2 == 0:
    print('You have entered an even number.')
else:
    print ('You have entered an odd number.')
```

Notice that the keyword **whille** is misspelled. If we try to run the program, we will get the following error:

```
C:Python34Scripts>python error.py
  File "error.py", line 3
    whille x%2 == 0:
        ^
```

```
SyntaxError: invalid syntax
```

2. Logical errors – also called **semantic errors**, logical errors cause the program to behave incorrectly, but they do not usually crash the program. Unlike a program with syntax errors, a program with logic errors can be run, but it does not operate as intended. Consider the following example of an logical error:

```
x = float(input('Enter a number: '))

y = float(input('Enter a number: '))


z = x+y/2

print ('The average of the two numbers you have entered is:',z)
```

The example above should calcuate the average of the two numbers the user enters. But, because of the order of operations in arithmetic (the division is evaluated before addition) the program will not give the right answer:

```
>>>

Enter a number: 3

Enter a number: 4

The average of the two numbers you have entered is: 5.0

>>>
```

To rectify this problem, we will simply add the parentheses: **z = (x+y)/2**

Now we will get the right result:

```
>>>

Enter a number: 3

Enter a number: 4

The average of the two numbers you have entered is: 3.5

>>>
```

The try...except statements

To handle errors (also known as exceptions) in Python, you can use the **try...except** statements. These statements tell Python what to do when an exception is encountered. This act of detecting and processing an exception is called **exception handling**. The syntax of the **try...except** statements is:

```
try:
```

```
    statements # statements that can raise exceptions
except:
    statements # statements that will be executed to handle exceptions
```

If an exception occurs, a **try** block code execution is stopped and an except block code will be executed. If no exception occurs inside the **try** block, the statements inside the **except** block will not be executed.

Consider the following example:

```
age=int(input('Enter your age: '))


if age <= 21:
    print('You are not allowed to enter, you are too young.')
else:
    print('Welcome, you are old enough.')
```

The example above asks the user to enter his age. It then checks to see if the user is old enough (older than 21). The code runs fine, as long as user enters only numberic values. However, consider what happens when the user enters a string value:

```
>>>
Enter your age: 13
You are not allowed to enter, you are too young.
>>> RESTART
>>>
Enter your age: 22
Welcome, you are old enough.
>>> RESTART
>>>
Enter your age: a
Traceback (most recent call last):
  File "C:/Python34/Scripts/exceptions.py", line 2, in <module>
    age=int(input('Enter your age: '))
ValueError: invalid literal for int() with base 10: 'a'
>>>
```

Because a numeric value is expected, the program crashed when the user entered a non-numeric value. We can use the **try…except** statements to recify this:

```
try:
    age=int(input('Enter your age: '))
except:
    print ('You have entered an invalid value.')
```

Now, the code inside the **try** block has its exceptions handled. If the user enters a non-numeric value, the statement inside the **except** block will be executed:

```
>>>
Enter your age: a
You have entered an invalid value.
>>>
```

In the example above the **except** clause catches all the exceptions that can occur, which is not considered a good programming practice. The **except** clause can have a specific exception associated, which we will describe in the following lessons.

The try…except…else statements

You can include an **else** clause when catching exceptions with a **try** statement. The statements inside the **else**block will be executed only if the code inside the **try** block doesn't generate an exception. Here is the syntax:

```
try:
    statements # statements that can raise exceptions
except:
    statements # statements that will be executed to handle exceptions
else:
    statements # statements that will be executed if there is no exception
```

Here is an example:

```
try:
    age=int(input('Enter your age: '))
except:
    print ('You have entered an invalid value.')
else:
```

```
    if age <= 21:
        print('You are not allowed to enter, you are too young.')
    else:
        print('Welcome, you are old enough.')
```

The output:

```
>>>
Enter your age: a
You have entered an invalid value.
>>> RESTART
>>>
Enter your age: 25
Welcome, you are old enough.
>>>RESTART
>>>
Enter your age: 13
You are not allowed to enter, you are too young.
>>>
```

As you can see from the output above, if the user enters a non-numeric value (in this case the letter **a**) the statement inside the **except** code block will be executed. If the user enters a numeric value, the statements inside the **else** code block will be executed.

The try…except…finally statements

You can use the **finally** clause instead of the **else** clause with a **try** statement. The difference is that the statements inside the **finally** block will always be executed, regardless whether an exception occurrs in the **try**block. Finally clauses are also called **clean-up** or **termination clauses**, because they are usually used when your program crashes and you want to perform tasks such as closing the files or logging off the user. Here is the syntax:

```
try:
    statements # statements that can raise exceptions
except:
    statements # statements that will be executed to handle exceptions
finally:
    statements # statements that will always be executed
```

Here is an example:

```
try:
age=int(input('Enter your age: '))
except:
print ('You have entered an invalid value.')
finally:
print ('There may or may not have been an exception.')
```

The output:

```
>>>
Enter your age: 55
There may or may not have been an exception.
>>> RESTART
>>>
Enter your age: a
You have entered an invalid value.
There may or may not have been an exception.
>>>
```

Note that the **print** statement inside the **finally** code block was executed regardless of whether the exception occured or not.

Catch specific exceptions

We've already mentioned that catching all exceptions with the **except** clause and handling every case in the same way is not considered to be a good programming practice. It is recommended to specify an exact exceptions that the **except** clause will catch. For example, to catch an exception that occurs when the user enters a non-numerical value instead of a number, we can catch only the built-in **ValueError** exception that will handle such event. Here is an example:

```
try:
    age=int(input('Enter your age: '))
except ValueError:
    print('Invalid value entered.')
else:
    if age >= 21:
        print('Welcome, you are old enough.')
```

```
    else:

        print('Go away, you are too young.')
```

The code above will ask the user for his age. If the user enters a number, the program will evaluate whether the user is old enough. If the user enters a non-numeric value, the **Invalid value entered** message will be printed:

```
>>>

Enter your age: 5

Go away, you are too young.

>>>RESTART

>>>

Enter your age: 22

Welcome, you are old enough.

>>>RESTART

>>>

Enter your age: a

Invalid value entered.

>>>
```

In the output above, you can see that the statements inside the **else** clause were executed when the user entered a number. However, when the user entered a non-numeric value (the letter **a**), the **ValueError** exception occured and the **print** statement inside the except **ValueError** clause was executed.

Note that the **except ValueError** clause will catch only exceptions that occur when the user enters a non-numeric value. If another exception occur, such as the **KeyboardInterrupt** exception (raised when the user hits **Ctrl+c**), the **except ValueError** block would not handle it. You can, however, specify multiple except clauses to handle multiple exceptions, like in this example:

```
try:

    age=int(input('Enter your age: '))

except ValueError:

    print('Invalid value entered.')

except KeyboardInterrupt:

    print('You have interrupted the program.')

else:

    if age >= 21:
```

```
        print('Welcome, you are old enough.')
    else:
        print('Go away, you are too young.')
```

The output:

```
>>>
Enter your age: 5
Go away, you are too young.
>>> RESTART
>>>
Enter your age: 22
Welcome, you are old enough.
>>>RESTART
>>>
Enter your age: a
Invalid value entered.
>>>
>>>
Enter your age:
You have interrupted the program.
>>>
```

You can also handle multiple exceptions with a single **except** clause. We can simple rewrite our program like this:

```
try:
    age=int(input('Enter your age: '))
except (ValueError, KeyboardInterrupt):
    print('There was an exception.')
else:
    if age >= 21:
        print('Welcome, you are old enough.')
    else:
        print('Go away, you are too young.')
```

Raise exception

You can manually throw (raise) an exception in Python with the keyword **raise**. This is usually done for the purpose of error-checking. Consider the following example:

```
try:
    raise ValueError
except ValueError:
    print('There was an exception.')
```

The code above demonstrates how to raise an exception. Here is the output:

```
>>>
There was an exception.
>>>
```

You can use the **raise** keyword to signal that the situation is exceptional to the normal flow. For example:

```
x = 5
if x < 10:
    raise ValueError('x should not be less than 10!')
```

Notice how you can write the error message with more information inside the parentheses. The example above gives the following output (by default, the interpreter will print a traceback and the error message):

```
>>>
Traceback (most recent call last):
  File "C:/Python34/Scripts/raise1.py", line 3, in <module>
    raise ValueError('x should not be less than 10!')
ValueError: x should not be less than 10!
>>>
```

Nest exception handling statements

Sometime, you need to place one exception-handling statement inside another. This process (called **nesting**) is often used in situations when you want to obtain the right type of user input. For example, if the user enters a non-numeric value instead of a number, you can give the user another chance to enter the right value type. Here is an example:

```
newChance = True

while newChance == True:
    try:
        age = int(input('Enter your age: '))
    except ValueError:
        print ('You have to enter a number!')
        try:
            startOver = int(input('To start over, enter 0. To exit, press any other key. '))
        except:
            print('OK, you do not want to start over, see you soon!')
            newChance = False
        else:
            if startOver == 0:
                newChance = True
            else:
                print('OK, you do not want to start over, see you soon!')
                newChance = False
```

The code above gives the user a second chance to enter a numeric value. The user can choose whether he wants to enter a new value. If the user enters **0**, he will get another chance to enter the right value. If he presses any other key, the **while** loop will end:

```
>>>
Enter your age: a
You have to enter a number!
To start over, enter 0. To exit, press any other key. r
OK, you do not want to start over, see you soon!
>>>RESTART
>>>
Enter your age: a
You have to enter a number!
To start over, enter 0. To exit, press any other key. 0
Enter your age: 21
```

Chapter 7 - Modules

In this chapter you will learn what modules are and how you can use them in your programs. You will also learn how to find files on your disk.

What are modules?

Modules in Python are separate code groupings which packages program code and data for reuse. Since modules are separate files, you need to tell Pthon where to find the file to read it into your application. This is usually done using the import or from statements.

Some of the advantages of using modules in your Python code are:

- they enable you to organize your code into smaller pieces that are easier to manage.

- the code in the modules can be reloaded and rerun as many times as needed, which enables code reuse.

- modules are self-contained – you can never see a name in another file, unless you explicitly import it. This helps you to avoid name clashes across your programs.

Commonly used modules that contain the source code for generic purposes are known as libraries.

Modules are usually stored in files with .py extension. The collection of classes, functions, and variables inside a module is known as attributes. These attributes can be accessed using their names.

Import modules

The most common way to create a module is to define a file with the .py extension that will contain the code you want to group separately from the rest of the application. In our example we will create a module with two simple functions. We will then import and use these functions in another file.

We will create a module with the following content:

```python
def Welcome(name):
    print ("Welcome", name)
    return


def Bye(name):
    print ("Bye", name)
    return
```

The module above contains two simple function that will print the supplied name, along with the greeting. If you follow along, make sure to save the module in the same directory that will also contain the top-level file.

There are two ways to import a module:

- using the IMPORT statement – imports the entire module.
- using the FROM…IMPORT statement – imports only individual module attributes.

Here is how we can import a module using the IMPORT statement:

```
import simple_module

simple_module.Welcome("Bob")
```

The first line (IMPORT SIMPLE_MODULE) imports the content of the file **simple_module.py**. The second line calls the function WELCOME and passes the string value of "**Bob**". Notice how we must precede the attribute name with the name of the module (without the .py extension). The result of the code above is:

```
>>>

Welcome Bob

>>>
```

We can also use the FROM…IMPORT statement to import only the attribute we need. Here is how it can be done:

```
from simple_module import Bye
```

When we import attributes using the FROM…IMPORT statement, we don't need to precede the attribute name with the name of the module:

```
>>> from simple_module import Bye

>>> Bye("John")

Bye John
```

However, if we try to call the WELCOME function, we will get an error, because only the BYE function was imported:

```
>>> Welcome("John")

Traceback (most recent call last):

File "<pyshell#5>", line 1, in <module>

Welcome("John")

NameError: name 'Welcome' is not defined

>>>
```

Find files on disk

Python looks for files using path information from three sources:

- **environment variables** – environment variables (such as PYTHONPATH) that containt a list of directories to search for files.

- **current directory** – Python can access files in contained in the current directory.

- **default directories** – Python can find files conteined in the set of default directories included in the path information.

To list your path information, the following code can be used:

```
import sys

for p in sys.path:
    print(p)
```

Here is the result:

```
>>>
C:/Python34/Scripts
C:\Python34\Scripts
C:\Python34\Lib\idlelib
C:\Windows\SYSTEM32\python34.zip
C:\Python34\DLLs
C:\Python34\lib
C:\Python34
C:\Python34\lib\site-packages
>>>
```

Your output will probably be different from the one above, depending on your Python version, OS version, etc.

To add a path to the **sys.path** attribute, use the following code:

```
import sys

sys.path.append("E:\\backup")

for p in sys.path:
    print(p)
```

The output of the code above:

```
>>>
```

```
C:/Python34/Scripts
C:\Python34\Scripts
C:\Python34\Lib\idlelib
C:\Windows\SYSTEM32\python34.zip
C:\Python34\DLLs
C:\Python34\lib
C:\Python34
C:\Python34\lib\site-packages
E:\backup
>>>
```

To change the current Python directory, the following code can be used:

```
import os
os.chdir("C:\Python34\Scripts")
```

Display module content

The module content is usually displayed using the dir () function, which displays the attributes provided by the module. Here is an example:

```
>>> import simple_module
>>> dir (simple_module)
['Bye', 'Welcome', '__builtins__', '__cached__', '__doc__', '__file__', '__loader__', '__name__', '__package__', '__spec__']
>>>
```

In the code above we have imported the module named SIMPLE_MODULE. We've then used the DIR () function to display the attributes provided by the module. Here is a brief description of the attributes:

- **Bye, Welcome** – the functions provided by the module
- **__builtins__** – a listing of all the built-in attributes that are accessible from the module.
- **__cached__** – the name and location of the cached file associated with the module.
- **__doc__** – help information for the module.
- **__file__** – the name and location of the module, relative to the current Python directory.
- **__loader__** – the loader information for this module.
- **__name__** – the name of the module.

- **__package__** – used internally by the import system.

- **__spec__** – set to the module spec that was used when importing the module.

You can get even more information about each attribute. For example, to display more information about the BYEfunction, we can use the following command:

```
>>> dir (simple_module.Bye)

['__annotations__', '__call__', '__class__', '__closure__', '__code__', '__defaults__',
'__delattr__', '__dict__', '__dir__', '__doc__', '__eq__', '__format__', '__ge__', '__get__',
'__getattribute__', '__globals__', '__gt__', '__hash__', '__init__', '__kwdefaults__', '__le__',
'__lt__', '__module__', '__name__', '__ne__', '__new__', '__qualname__', '__reduce__',
'__reduce_ex__', '__repr__', '__setattr__', '__sizeof__', '__str__', '__subclasshook__']

>>>
```

Chapter 8 - Strings

In this chapter we will describe what strings are. You will also learn some useful string functions and how to escape characters in Python.

What are strings?

In Python, strings are used to store a contiguous set of characters. Strings are one of the most popular data types in Python and can be defined in three ways:

- **using single quotes** – for example:

```
>>> print ('Hello World!')
Hello World!
```

- **using double quotes** – for example:

```
>>> print ("Hello World!")
Hello World!
```

- **using triple double or single quotes** – the triple quotes enable you to define strings spanning multiple lines. For example:

```
>>> print ('''Hello world!
This is a new line.''')
Hello world!
This is a new line.
>>>
```

The reason why both the single and double quotes are used is so you can embed a quote character of the other type inside a string. For example, you may embed a single-quote character in a string enclosed in double-quote characters:

```
>>> newString = "Mark's car"
>>> print (newString)
Mark's car
```

Escape characters

Let's say that we want to print the path to the directory **C:\nature**. Consider what happens when we try to print the path:

```
>>> print ("C:\nature")
C:
ature
```

In the example above, Python interpreted the **\n** characters as special characters. These characters are not meant to be displayed on the screen; they are used to control the display. In our case, the **\n** characters were interpreted as a new line.

The **backslash (\)** character is used in Python to escape special characters. So in our example, we would use the following code to print the path:

```
>>> print ("C:\\nature")
C:\nature
```

Here is another example. What if we have a string that uses double-quotes and you want to put a double-quote inside the string:

```
>>> print ("She said: "I don't love you anymore"")


SyntaxError: invalid syntax
```

In the example above, Python thinks that the second double quote ends the string. To rectify this, we need to escape the double quotes inside the string with backslash:

```
>>> print ("She said: \"I don't love you anymore\"")
She said: "I don't love you anymore"
```

Access individual characters

We've already learned that strings are made of a contiguous set of characters. You can access individual characters in a string or obtain a range of characters in a string. Here is how it can be done:

```
>>> newString='Hello world!'
>>> print (newString[0])
H
```

In the example above we've created a string variable **newString** with the value of '**Hello world!**'. We've then accessed the first character of the string using the square brackets. Since Python strings are zero-based (meaning that they start with 0), we got the letter **H**.

Here is another example. To obtain the letter **w**, we can use the following code:

```
>>> print (newString[6])
w
```

As you can see from the output above, the white space is also interpreted as a character. That is why we've used the number **6** in the square brackets.

To obtain a range of characters from a string, we need to provide the beginning and ending letter count in the square brackets. Here is an example:

```
>>> print (newString[0:3])
```

```
Hel
```

Notice how the character at the index **3** was not included in the output. The second number specifies the first character that you don't want to include.

You can leave out the beginning or ending number in a range and get the reminder of the string:

```
>>> print (newString[:5])
Hello
>>> print (newString[5:])
world!
```

If you want to start counting from the end of the string, you can use a negative index. The index of **-1** includes the right-most character of the string:

```
>>> print (newString[-1])
!
```

String functions

Python offers a lot of functions that enable you to modify strings. For example, there are functions to transform all characters in a string to uppercase, obtain the length of a string, strip leading and trailing spaces in a string, etc. Here is a brief description of some of the commonly used functions:

- **capitalize()** – capitalizes the first letter of a string.
- **isdigit()** – returns True if a string contains only digits.
- **islower()** – returns True if all alphabetic characters are in lowercase.
- **len(string)** – obtains the length of string.
- **lower()** – converts all uppercase letters to lowercase.
- **upper()** – converts all lowercase letters to uppercase.
- **strip()** – strips all leading and trailing whitespace characters.
- **swapcase()** – inverts the case of each alphabetic character.

Here are a couple of examples:

```
>>> newString='Hello world!'
>>> len(newString)
12
>>> newString.isdigit()
```

```
False
>>> newString.islower()
False
>>> newString.lower()
'hello world!'
>>> newString.swapcase()
'hELLO WORLD!'
```

Search strings

There are many functions in Python to search strings for specific information. Here are some of them:

- **count(value)** – counts how many times the value in the parenthesis appear in a string.

- **endswith(value)** – returns True if a string ends with the value specified in the parenthesis.

- **find(value)** – searches the string for a value specified in the parenthesis and outputs the index of the location.

- **replace(old, new)** – replaces all occurances of old with new.

Here are a couple of examples:

```
>>> newString='Hello world!'
>>> newString.count('world')
1
>>> newString.endswith('!')
True
>>> newString.find('llo')
2
>>> newString.replace('Hello', 'Bye')
'Bye world!'
```

www.ingramcontent.com/pod-product-compliance
Lightning Source LLC
Chambersburg PA
CBHW060457060326
40689CB00020B/4559